£2.00

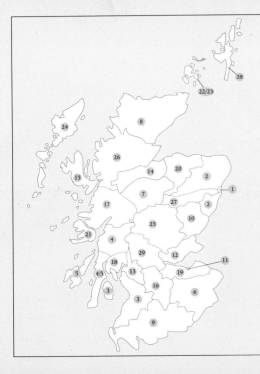

1. Aberdeen
2. Aberdeenshire
3. Arran & Ayrshire
4. Argyll
5. Southern Argyll
6. The Borders
7. The Cairngorms
8. Caithness & Sutherland
9. Dumfries and Galloway
10. Dundee & Angus
11. Edinburgh
12. Fife, Kinross & Clackmannan
13. Glasgow
14. Inverness

15. The Isle of Skye
16. Lanarkshire
17. Lochaber
18. Loch Lomond, Cowal & Bute
19. The Lothians
20. Moray
21. Mull & Iona
22. Orkney
23. Orkney in Wartime
24. The Outer Hebrides
25. Perthshire
26. Ross & Cromarty
27. Royal Deeside
28. Shetland
29. Stirling & The Trossachs

The remaining four books, Caledonia, Distinguished Distilleries, Scotland's Mountains and Scotland's Wildlife feature locations throughout the country so are not included in the above list.

SCOTLAND'S WILDLIFE

NESS PUBLISHING

2 Silhouetted red deer.

SCOTLAND'S WILDLIFE

Welcome to my world!

In world, or even European terms, Scotland is a small country. And yet compared to so many others of much greater size, it packs a much greater punch when it comes to biodiversity. This is partly explained by the UK's geographical position off the western seaboard of Europe and under the maritime influence of the Atlantic Ocean, where predominately westerly-driven weather systems ensure that we have a milder climate compared to many other parts of the world at the same latitude. Scotland also has an east-west division due to the effects of the warming Gulf Stream sweeping around the west coast, but which leaves the east open to the influence of much colder continental weather systems coming in from Europe. Rainfall figures are markedly different between, say, Fort William in the west and Nairn in the east which claims to be the sunniest place in Scotland! While all that rain may seem a disadvantage to many visitors, it is these very conditions which have created and sustain fantastic habitats such as the western oak and hazel woodlands. But travel just 60-80 miles east into the Cairngorm Mountains and we enter a radically different, sub-arctic environment. So, the diversity of the climate leads to diversity of habitats which in turn support a vast range of specialised plant and animal life. Perhaps only in Scotland do you find palm trees and arctic plants living in a closeness of proximity that would be unfeasible anywhere else.

4   Sometimes referred to as 'tysties', black guillemots can often be found nesting on man-made structures around our coast, such as in the crevices of stone piers and harbour walls.

From summer through to late autumn, Atlantic salmon make their epic journeys from the ocean to the upper reaches of rivers to breed, negotiating waterfalls along the way.

Over the centuries, many of these habitats have been greatly altered by humans, most notably by the reduction of natural forest cover. The once great Caledonian pine forest is a prime example, with less than five percent of the original forest remaining in scattered fragments. But attitudes are changing and we are seeing long-term initiatives by organisations such as Trees for Life to restore these native woodlands. In time, and when these habitats are large and rich enough, it is conceivable that some of the large carnivores such as wolves and brown bears could be reintroduced. In the meantime, the reintroduction of red kites and white-tailed sea eagles are two examples that clearly demonstrate the benefits in bringing back these lost species, not just in terms of increasing biodiversity, but also in the effect it can have on both local communities and tourism. Whether it be otters, puffins, golden eagles or leaping salmon, there has always been a sense of pride in having these charismatic species as neighbours. Another aspect to enjoyment and

6   Also known as blue hares, mountain hares aren't necessarily found only on the highest parts of the hills. Numbers vary enormously with peaks and troughs every decade or so.

wonder of the Scottish landscape and its wildlife is the feeling of being in wild and relatively unpolluted environments. There is also the sense of adventure to be had in going in search of wildlife, particularly when it involves travelling to remote locations. Whatever the season, habitat or even time of day, the natural history of the Scottish landscape always provides surprises; it's just a case of spending time in the field to look.

This book has been organised by groups of species. As Scotland is particularly rich in bird species, these have been divided up so as to achieve variety as you turn the pages. So we begin with birds that range from the mountains and moors to coastal wetlands, then turn to Scotland's mammals, again organised by habitat from land to sea, which in turn leads into the section on seabirds, followed by creatures of the shore, and so on. There are even reptiles! All in all, Scotland is home to a fantastic concoction of all creatures great and small!

With their somewhat comical appearance, puffins must be our most popular seabird but it is not until they are seen in close-up that we discover how small they are - just 25cms tall.

8   The sights and sounds of a black grouse 'lek' in spring are spectacular. It occurs early in the morning at traditional sites where males display and compete with each other to attract females.

The red grouse of our heather moors are actually a subspecies of the more northern willow grouse.
Famous as a game bird, large tracts of land are managed to boost their numbers.

10 Despite their huge size, capercaillies can be difficult to spot when they are high up in the Scots pines where they feed mostly upon pine needles in the native pine forests.

Seldom found below 600 metres, ptarmigan are one of Scotland's hardiest birds and able to endure **11** the worst of weather. Like stoats and mountain hares, they turn white in winter.

12 With long, curved bills for probing the ground for prey, curlews are the largest wading bird in Europe. They spend the winter around the coast but move to upland areas to nest in spring.

Female dotterel are much more brightly coloured than the males and even display to them before **13** leaving them to incubate their eggs alone. A real case of role reversal!

14 Dippers are full of character and capable of diving and walking around under water in shallow fast flowing streams and rivers where they hunt for aquatic invertebrates.

Changing farming practices affect the fortunes of birds. Lapwings may still find suitable arable and grass **15** fields but corncrakes are more specialised, relying on traditional hay meadows and rough grassland.

16 Ringed and golden plovers, though similar in name, require different habitats in the breeding season. Ringed plovers are rarely found away from the coast but golden plovers prefer uplands and mountains.

The colour of the legs of greenshanks and redshanks are a descriptive clue to differentiate between these two species of waders, but greenshanks are much rarer and in the UK only nest on Scottish hills. **17**

18 Widely distributed across marine and freshwater wetlands in Scotland, grey herons are renowned for their patience and stealth when stalking their prey.

Apart from the seashore and gravel beds by upland streams, oystercatchers also nest is some very **19**
odd places, such as on flat roofs, roundabouts, and once in a flowerbed at an airport!

20 Living up to their name, turnstones do indeed turn over small stones and pebbles when searching for invertebrate food but they will also rummage through dead seaweed too.

Left: common blue damselflies are both blue and the most abundant species of damselfly in the UK. **21**
Right: golden-ringed dragonflies are very striking and are the longest dragonflies in the UK.

22 Scottish wildcats are highly endangered, primarily through inter-breeding with feral domestic cats. A defining feature of a true wildcat is their thick, club-shaped striped tail.

Scottish wildcats tend to look much sleeker in summer in their thinner coat but in autumn their **23**
thicker winter coat develops and they can look like a very different animal.

24 Because of their rarity, pine martens were once described as a 'mythical' animal but their range has expanded from their stronghold in Wester Ross to much of Scotland now.

Stoats are often confused with weasels, but they are larger and have a distinctive black tip to the end **25** of their tails. A large proportion of stoats also turn snow-white in winter.

26 The red fox wasn't particularly common in the Highlands until large-scale sheep farming began. In many areas their earths are more likely to be in rock dens than in burrows.

The best conditions for watching badgers are calm, still evenings when it is cloudy and without a full moon. Unfortunately, this coincides with peak activity of biting midges! 27

28 The most reliable places to see otters in Scotland are any quiet sea loch on the west coast of Scotland, the Hebridean Isles and Shetland Isles. Look for them on a falling tide.

Extinct in Scotland for over 400 years, the reintroduction of beavers must be welcomed because the **29** wetland habitats they create benefit so many other species.

30 Few Scottish water voles fit the storybook image of Ratty from *Wind in the Willows*. Instead, they have black coats and live in small burns (streams) high up on moors and mountains.

The 'tribes' of feral goats scattered around Scotland are descended from domesticated stock. **31**
After several generations in the wild, they revert back to growing shaggy coats and longer horns.

32 Competition from increasing numbers of grey squirrels has affected the population of native red squirrels and it is now rare to see them in deciduous woodland in southern Scotland.

Red squirrels that gather fallen cones often prefer to feed on stumps or small raised hummocks **33** where, after they have gone, it's possible to see the tell-tale signs of their presence.

34 Starting in late September and ending by the second week of October, the red deer rutting season is a time when the bellowing of roaring stags echoes in the glens.

The red deer that we see on open hills were in fact originally woodland mammals and those still **35** found living in forests grow bigger, thanks to the better feeding and shelter.

36 Autumn is when red deer are in peak condition and those that have fed well in the summer months stand the best chance of surviving the long highland winter.

Red deer calves in Scotland are generally born from late May until mid June. In the early weeks, **37** the calves have spotted coats which help to camouflage them from predators.

38 Although not as conspicuous as herds of red deer living on open hills, the beautiful slender roe deer is officially now the commonest species of deer living in Scotland.

Reintroduced to Scotland in 1952, the Cairngorm reindeer herd has flourished ever since and **39** guided tours are run daily to allow visitors to see them in their mountain habitat.

40 Like stoats, mountain hares are the only UK species of mammal that turns white in winter. An adaptation for camouflage, this is obviously a disadvantage when there is little snow.

Despite their name, common seals, or more correctly harbour seals, are actually fewer in number **41** than grey seals and their pups are born in summer rather than winter.

42 Scotland holds internationally important numbers of grey seals. The white coats of pups (born in October) are a throwback from times when they offered camouflage in snow and ice.

Sometimes known as rookeries, the breeding grounds where grey seals come ashore to give birth are **43** often on remote beaches, at the foot of cliffs or on uninhabited islands.

44 Chanonry Point by the village of Fortrose on the Moray Firth remains one of the best shore-based sites in Europe to see a resident population of Bottlenose dolphins.

The waters around the Hebrides are rich in marine life and in mid to late summer, when the **45** mackerel shoals are at their greatest, minke whales move in to feed.

46 Named after their rhythmic call, kittiwakes are cliff-nesting gulls that, outside the breeding season, spend most of their lives on the sea and out in the Atlantic in winter.

Fulmars are actually related to albatrosses rather than gulls and behave similarly in flight, **47** gliding low over the surface of the sea, only occasionally needing to flap their wings.

48 Gannets use what is commonly known as the 'plunge diving' method of fishing, striking the water at around 60 miles per hour and reaching prey down to a depth of ten metres.

With a 150,000 birds, the Bass Rock in the Firth of Forth holds the world's largest population of **49** Northern gannets. Their Latin name 'Morus bassanus' is derived from the site.

50 Puffins belong to the group of seabirds known as auks and the one thing that they have in common is that they all have short wings, but despite this they are very fast fliers.

Puffins nest in burrows and although they are capable of excavating these in soft soil, they will also **51** make use of those made by rabbits or gaps under and between boulders.

52 Unusually for a water-bird, cormorants must periodically leave the water to dry out their plumage which explains why they are often seen perched with wings outstretched.

Slimmer, and more slightly built than cormorants, shags are really beautiful seabirds in close-up **53** with a rich, glossy dark green plumage and crest.

54 Recent research has shown that arctic terns migrate much further than first thought.
With a lifespan of around thirty years, they may clock up one-and- a-half million miles.

As its name suggests, greater black-backed gulls are large, thick-set powerful seabirds and, although **55** they are capable of overpowering prey, they also feed on carrion.

56 Left: guillemots nest in dense colonies on sea cliffs and stacks. They do not build nests but lay their eggs, that are pointed at one end to prevent them rolling away, on bare rock. Right: a bridled guillemot.

Guillemots and razorbills can usually be found nesting alongside each other. To tell them apart, **57** razorbills have shorter, thicker beaks and darker plumage.

58 The island of Rum holds the world's largest breeding colony of Manx shearwaters, but in daytime you might never know because they only return to land under cover of darkness.

Red-breasted mergansers are one of a group of three species in the UK known as 'saw-billed' ducks, **59**
due to their serrated bills which have evolved to grasp slippery fish.

60 Black-throated divers are a beautifully marked and endangered species of water-bird that nests only in the north-west Highlands on large freshwater lochs and reservoirs.

The plumage of red-throated divers changes from summer to winter but a key indentifying feature **61** is their slightly up-turned bill.

62 After years of persecution, greylag geese were once limited to the north-west Highlands and it was from this population that eggs were removed to re-establish it as a resident UK bird.

Like greylags, pink-footed geese are often referred to as 'grey geese'. These winter visitors arrive **63** in large numbers and can be found roosting on lochs and estuaries.

64 Barnacle geese are highly sociable, attractive geese and two of the best places to see them in Scotland are on the Isle of Islay and at Caerlaverock on the Solway coast of Dumfriesshire.

The Scottish coastline holds most of the UK population of eiders, our heaviest and fastest-flying species of duck. These seagoing birds feed upon shellfish, such as mussels.

66 Unlike many species of duck, male and female shelduck both have eye-catching plumage. The reason is that they nest in burrows so the female does not need to be camouflaged.

Goldeneye ducks were traditionally a winter visitor to the UK until 1970 when a pair bred in
Scotland. Encouraged by tree-mounted nest boxes, there is now a small resident population.

68 With fewer than thirty pairs of Slavonian grebes breeding in the UK, and only in Scotland, these beautiful birds can be seen in spring and summer at the RSPB's reserve of Loch Ruthven near Inverness.

Apart from a handful of resident breeding birds, all whooper swans in Scotland are winter visitors from **69** Iceland. A good place to see them is Insh Marshes Bird Reserve near Kingussie in the Cairngorms.

70 Left: from a worldwide total of around 1,500 species of starfish, 32 occur in UK waters. Many can live longer than one might expect, often between 10 and 30 years. Right: oar weed, a type of seaweed.

The clean, pristine waters around much of the Scottish coast explain the rich diversity of life that **71** we see on our shore. Upper left: sea anemone; upper right: sea urchin; below: moon jellyfish.

72 Anyone who has spent time rock-pooling is very likely to have come across a shore crab hiding beneath a rock. The redder, edible crab is found in deeper waters offshore.

Atlantic salmon have been recorded spawning from October to February and all return to do so in the river of their birth. They identify it by the taste of the water.

74 After a decline due to pesticides in the 1950s, peregrine numbers have increased and they are now even found in urban environments nesting on tall buildings. Right: adult and large chick.

White-tailed sea eagles have become much less wary of people in tour boats. Nowadays visitors can obtain close-up views of the ease with which they can snatch fish from the surface of the sea.

76 Golden eagles rank as the most popular species of bird that visitors to Scotland wish to see; it is perhaps their elusive nature that makes it all the more rewarding when it happens.

The eyries of golden eagles are often built on north-facing cliffs, crags and gullies so that the eaglets are in shade for much of the day and not vulnerable to dehydration.

78 Extinct as a breeding bird in Scotland in the late 19th century, a reintroduction programme for red kites began in 1989 and they can now be enjoyed in many parts of Scotland.

Common buzzards perched on roadside telegraph poles and the like are often mistaken for golden eagles, hence their nickname, 'tourists' eagles'!

80 Scotland is a stronghold for the rare and specially protected hen harrier. In spring and summer, look for them on upland areas of moor with scrubby grassland.

Sparrowhawks were once regarded as rather uncommon but the population is thankfully now **81** recovering and more people have the opportunity to see these beautiful birds.

82 Merlins are the UK's smallest bird of prey. They are as at home on the coast in winter feeding on waders as they are on uplands in spring and summer where they target meadow pipits.

The RSPB reserve of Loch Garten on Strathspey was the first place where ospreys returned to breed **83** in the UK in 1959. Now they are well established across much of Scotland.

84 Both tawny and barn owls are reasonably widespread across much of Scotland but the rarer barn owl (left) is the one more likely to be seen hunting at dusk. Tawny owls are strictly nocturnal.

Of all our species of owl, short-eared owls are the one most likely to been seen flying in daylight. **85**
In winter, look for them hunting over rough grassland and coastal marshes.

86 Commonly known as 'Bonxies', great skuas are large, bold birds capable of killing smaller birds such as puffins but will equally follow fishing boats for a free handout.

Arctic skuas occur in both light and dark forms and obtain much of their food by harassing other seabirds until they drop their catch.

88 The Northern raven is one of the earliest-nesting birds in Scotland, with many incubating eggs by the end of February. More notable perhaps, is their rasping caw, cawing calls.

Jays are a member of the crow family, also known as 'corvids'. All are more intelligent than any other species of bird and their wariness makes it difficult to get close to them.

90 Much maligned, adders are well able to avoid contact with people, both by 'tasting' the air for scent, and because they are highly sensitive to ground vibrations.

Common lizards are also known as 'viviparous' lizards, a term meaning 'to bear live young'. **91**
They lay 'eggs' but these only have a thin membrane from which the young emerge.

92 Birds migrate to Scotland, either in winter to escape harsher conditions further north, such as waxwings (left), or in the summer to breed and where there is a good supply of food, such as wheatear (right).

Scotland's big birds get lots of attention, but our tiny birds are no less worthy of it for their beautiful **93** plumage and, in some cases, their rarity. Clockwise from top left: goldcrest, crested tit, crossbill, siskin.

94 Left: typically nesting in gorse thickets, stonechats can really stand out because of their habit of perching on fences or stems of vegetation that they use as lookout posts for prey. Right: redstart.

Starlings are still one of the UK's commonest garden birds. In autumn they form huge communal roosts in woodlands and reedbeds. The spectacular event pictured is called a murmuration.

Published 2016 by Ness Publishing, 47 Academy Street, Elgin, Moray, IV30 1LR.
Phone 01343 549663 www.nesspublishing.co.uk

Text and photographs © Laurie Campbell
www.lauriecampbell.com

ISBN 978-1-906549-44-2

Front cover: otter; p.1: white-tailed bumble bee; this page: slow worm; back cover: golden eagle

For more about Laurie Campbell, please see over > > > >

As a self-taught naturalist and one of Scotland's best known natural history and landscape photographers, Laurie Campbell was honoured with the **Lifetime Achievement Award** at the third annual RSPB Nature of Scotland Awards in November 2014. After graduating with a degree in photography at Napier University in 1985, Laurie became Scotland's first full-time professional nature photographer. Since then he has dedicated over 35 years to photographing Scotland's distinctive wildlife and flora. His archive of over 180,000 images is the largest of any single photographer specialising in recording Scottish flora, fauna and landscape. In recognition of the effect that his photography has had, he was voted to be included in 'Highland Naturalists', an exhibition staged at Great Glen House, Scottish Natural Heritage's headquarters in Inverness. The exhibition featured 30 people from the past 300 years whose work has significantly contributed to the understanding and enjoyment of natural history in the Scottish Highlands.

All of the images in this book are available as limited-edition, A3-sized prints which Laurie hand prints using archival inks and papers. For information about the prints and to purchase copies, Laurie may be contacted by email at:

laurie@lauriecampbell.com
www.lauriecampbell.com